Multitude of Blessings

Testimonies of Faith and Works

Jonathan L Taylor

How does God speak to you?

Follow this man's journey that proves God's love and
Faithfulness to those who abide by the teachings of
Jesus Christ.

See the rewards that come from Faith and Works.

Enjoy Multiple Blessings

My Favorite Bible Verse.
John 3-16

DEDICATION

It was all Jesus! It had nothing to do with anyone else,
Dedicated to the Glory of Jesus Christ

Verses quoted are from the following Bible Versions:
ASV American Standard
CSB Christian Standard Bible
ESV English Standard Version
KJV King James Version
NIV New International Version
NLT New Living Translation
NTE New Testament for Everyone

Cover Photos by *Jeff Jacobs*. See his work on Pixabay
Guest Editor and Cover Design: Claudette Osborne

CONTENTS

1   Having Given Thy Home to the Lord   2

2   The Lord's Perfect Painting   11

3   Restored Faith   19

4   A Boost of Faith   25

5   Uplifting of Hope   30

Location: Jacobs Well, TX
Living a life of obedience to the teaching of
Jesus Christ, our Lord and Savior.

CHAPTER 1
HAVING GIVEN THY HOME TO THE LORD

Written August 6, 2017

Around March of 2015, the Holy Spirit of God had said me, "Give your home fully furnished through the church, to a needy family." These were His exact words! Instantly my answer to him was YES. Despite four years prior, I had been taken advantage of by not only family but also friends and the one I was going to marry. However, I was able to work much and pay off half of a two-bedroom two-bath home, fully furnished with new furnishings in two years. It was not too bad for a 35-year-old who had recently given up all friends and family and turned to the Lord for the first time. I questioned the Lord as to who might genuinely deserve all thy accomplishments. The response was: "For your Pastor at church if he doesn't know of someone now, in the future, he will" Wow, what powerful words from God Himself! Who was I to do this? What would happen? I will unfold for you all, many Miracles, Signs, Wonders, and Healings that I can testify of. At that time, I was stepping into I did not understand.

"Give, and it will be given to you. A good measure, pressed down, shaken together, and running over. For the measure you use, it will be measured to you".
(Luke 6:38)

All the following events I am sharing to the world confirm that God Is an Awesome and Mighty Man of His Word! AMEN!

At the time, I heard the word of the Lord as a single striving man of Church, that was self-employed, and running my household of two dogs, two cats, two parrots, and taking care of myself. I had purchased thirteen acres of property that required ample work to be done. I was in the midst of finally concluding, "what the heck am I doing?" There is no way I can do all this alone. Then the Lord spoke and said to me "gift thy home". The very next day, I grabbed my deed and I headed to my Church, Floresville Christian Fellowship Church, in big Floresville, Texas. I called my Pastor Benny Herrera and awaited him on the front steps of our Church. I told him the words the Lord gave me, and with that, I handed him my house and property deed and said, "I hereby sacrifice my home and everything in it, TO BE RICH AT HEART!" Most did not know that for years I had a broken, bleeding, and hardened heart. For two months, only the pastors knew of this and were instructed to pray for the right people to come along, the ones whom the Lord wanted to receive this home.

In perspective, the home is fully furnished meaning new furniture, flat screen TVs, a fridge, a dishwasher, a flat top stove, a washer, a dryer, a business computer, a desk, a laser printer, dishes, a 130-gallon fish tank with fish, a newly built back covered deck, an operational hot tub and a lot more was given. *Just so the grounds are set straight, it was not a rundown home with a lot of old trash.* I had spent a total of two years remodeling and getting things how I wanted, being this was my first and only home in my thirty-five years of my life.

Thus, Starts an Outpouring Of the Spirit

A few days after giving the deed to my pastor, I had woken in the morning with a pressing sensation on my head and was confused for days. It took me a while to understand what had happened. The four/five years of my bleeding, broken, and hardened heart was gone!

And as my company shirts say, "Fixing Everything Except Broken Hearts, That's GOD'S Job."

"He heals the brokenhearted and binds up their wounds"
(Psalm 147:3)

Yes, He does and AMEN, thank you, Jesus! This is just the start of what was to unfold in my Christian walk with the Lord. As I was still living in the house, awaiting whom it may be given to, more things started to happen. One morning I had no hope, no will press on that day. On an average day, I wake up at 4 am, shower, and read at least one passage in the Holy Bible. This morning, I did not even have the strength to shower. I was so conflicted. I shot up, took a quick shower, put on clean clothes, and made myself read just one paragraph. That is all I needed to do, and I wish I remember what was in the paragraph. To my surprise, I looked down and saw a single tiny wing resting on my pant leg, above the knee. It was about the size of a pinky fingernail if you will, and wow, like most beetle wings are brilliant with color. Although I only had one light on in the house so many colors glistened out of its clearwing. Like you know, if you hold a diamond up to the light or even a prism, these are the colors I saw! Then the Holy Spirit of God said, "Pick it up," and so I did. With this wing on my index finger, I marveled at the color shining out of it. Then I felt the Spirit in me guide me to blow it off my finger. Amazing, as I did just that, that one wing was now seven. All seven were spinning, the wing attachment side down, evenly spaced, and hovered directly in front of me. They slowly descended to the ground. The Lord Says

"There are different kinds of gifts. But they are all given to believers by the same Spirit" (Corinthians 12:4). "All the gifts are produced by one and the same Spirit. He gives gifts to each person, just as He decides"
(1 Corinthians 12:11.) Amen, Amen, and Amen!

God is amazing, and this is just a start as to what has unfolded in this single testimony. As you continue this journey, with Christ Jesus and me, note I had no clue that any of these things would happen nor were even possible. But as I do know now,

> *"Jesus Looked at them and said, "With man this is impossible, but with God all things are possible"*
> *(Matthew 19:26)*

Years before having received this Gift of The Spirit, people generally would pass by, unaware of my presence. Even the people I tried being around never seemed to notice of me. This treatment was horrible, a true struggle and test. The first thing I realized the following day while entering a grocery store was that every head turned, and most people started to migrate toward me. I freaked out, stopped my shopping, made a beeline to the door, and went straight home. I locked my front gate and door, as usual, then I turned my phone off. I sat there, wondering, what had changed? Ah, I was given *a Gift* from The Holy Spirit of GOD! Even the church members at service kept saying, *"What have you changed? There is a radiant glow around you."* After a while, I responded, it is the Lord in me. I was full of The Holy Ghost, Hallelujah! Amen, Brothers and Sisters.

> *"All of them were filled with the Holy Spirit and began to speak in other tongues as the Spirit enabled them". (Acts 2:4)*

The Receiving of Thy Home Given

It was roughly two months after I had given my pastor the deed. Several pastors had prayed for the correct people to come along, as the Lord had instructed. An issue arose while a dedicated man of our Church was cutting the grass of the grounds. My pastor told me that the brother came to him with the intent of quitting the Church, to stop helping the local elderly and giving up on God. He and his wife had dedicated four years to serving this Church and community while holding their full-time jobs. Then I found out that four years ago, they had given up their home to someone in Texas. After four years of serving the Church, they stilled lived in an apartment, trying desperately to buy a house out of town near their sister. The sister I was aware of needed spiritual help due to the enemy attacking her by seeing her dead mother's images in the house. I know personally that these things happen. I overcame eight months of a tortuous living hell, seeing demons, devils, and having physical attacks. These attacks do happen as I can testify. The only way to battle these things is having the word of the Lord, for His word IS a Double Edge Sword that defeats the enemy and his strongholds!

"For the word of God is quick, and powerful, and sharper than any two-edged sword, piercing even to the dividing asunder of soul and spirit, and the joints and marrow, and is a discerner of the thoughts and intents of the heart". (Hebrews 4:12) Amen

It was enlightening to hear their story. Not only did this husband and wife give their home away, but they, while living in an apartment, had been donating their belongings in storage to the elderly, poor, and needy. Things such as, i.e., washer, dryer, fridge, etc. So my pastor's side of the story continues; the brother came to me saying, "We have done all these good things for God, God's House, God's people, and we have had nothing good come out of it in four years". It was then that the pastor realized who the home was intended to be given to. Pastor's words, "you need to get your wife and meet me in my office now," regarding giving up on the Lord. AS the husband and wife sat at the pastor's desk, he reached in his desk drawer and pulled the deed to the property and fully furnished home. He said, "It appears to me that this is meant for you both this entire time"! This is so awesome to experience. I am telling you that this family gave much, and through obedience, listening, and doing for the Lord, they received much. Yes, and AMEN!

"Give generously to him and do without a grudging heart; then because of this, the Lord your God will bless you in all your work and in everything you put your hand too" (Deuteronomy 15:10)

OK, this is cool, someone listens and gives not only a home but also most of their belongings in the hope of future prosperity. Due to my obedience and doing the Lord's will, they were able to receive a house *fully furnished*, plus some. An awesome testimony, but it gets even better! As I met this couple so that I could sign over the paperwork, the wife clutched her husband, almost collapsing. Then she said, "Do you remember that sister I spoke of that needed spiritual help?" I said, yes. She informed me, "That sister, my sister and her family, live two blocks from this house we just received!" Oh my word, so is it faithfulness that allowed them to receive a free fully furnished home and put them two blocks from their sister, YES and AMEN, Glory to God.

(Proverbs 21:26) *the righteous gives and does not hold back.*

A Continued Outpouring of the Spirit

This testimony of God's greatness does not stop yet. I now had a deadline to get out of the home, although I bought 13 acres that required one year of cleaning up, with 2 acres being a dump. I had a 10'x16' storage shed built amid the dump so that I had a roof over my head. So yes, I sacrificed everything to move into a shed where I lived for an added 1.5 years, with my loved ones: Two cats, two dogs, and two parrots. It had an outdoor shower, with an outdoor toilet, that I made.

It was not too bad aside from not having water for two months, and in the winter, I could shower at Church. But as the single man that I am, I will survive. It was like, as I told people, "high-class camping." At that time, somewhere around March of 2016, I decided to quit smoking, since I had no real reason to do it anymore as I was having shortness of breath, wheezing, etc. To my surprise, on the third night of having quit smoking, I felt a power come over me, and I could feel myself being pulled across my bed as I awoke that morning! I was baffled. I could breathe perfectly fine, no wheezing, no shortness of breath. The more I would breathe, I was getting dizzy and lightheaded. Then the Lord Spoke, "Your lungs are renewed, you no longer need to take deep breaths" Another Healing, Thank You, Jesus!

(Psalm 103:2-3) *Bless the Lord, O my soul, and forget none of His benefits; Who pardons all your iniquities, Who heals all your diseases*. Amen.

Despite my struggles in the life of loneliness, I know God is with me, and the only thing in life needed to live is His Grace! As I struggled with my living conditions, I continued helping my Church, helping others, continued self-employment and cleaning up my property. After one year of cleaning up the property, I had a vision of building a home, despite having given all my money away that I may have paid to have to build a new home. I would spend the next year working week after week to slowly build my own home, even after working all day. During that time, I had overworked myself causing my right ankle to tear. Though being the hard-headed man, I never went to a doctor nor stopped what I was doing. Day after day, my one day after church service, I was lying in my shack, when *I felt a coolness of the Heavens open over my back. I had a two-time broken ribs that I never took care and it started to heal*.

"So, I prophesied as I was commanded. And as I was prophesying, there was a noise, a rattling sound, and the bones came together, bone to bone. I looked, and tendons and flesh appeared on them, and skin covered them" (Ezekiel 37:7)

With this scripture in mind, I heard my bone and flesh growing back right in front of me! Painful, yes! It lasted a few hours to the point of passing out. The next morning, I got out of bed feeling better and stronger than ever. I had no more pain in the twice-broken ribs.

A week or so later, the same thing happened to my injured ankle, it was an enormous pain for quite a while then the next day, pain-free. Wow, is the Lord healing and/or renewing my broken mind, heart, body, and soul? The answer is Most Definitely! In December 2016, I had moved from my box to my 2,500 square foot home even though it still was not finished, it was perfectly livable. It lacked a bit of sheetrock and painting, but it has been one heck of an accomplishment. And time and time again, the Lord has granted me strength and wisdom to be able to build a home from merely jotting it on paper. This year of 2017, I have backed off the home to serve the Lord and His house. I have been asked by the Good Lord this year to gift much more; indeed, I have, much more I had done and given the Lord and His people when he asked me. HE gave me many more testimonies. Many more beautiful stories of Healing the Broken, Lifting of Broken Spirits, and more families that are receiving from the Lord through their faithfulness. The Lord has shown me much including, but not limited to: Angels, Heaven, Demons, and Weapons of Spiritual War. There is much going on around us that we are not meant to see. There is not only war here on Earth, but also war in the heavens. Prepare yourselves Saints if you are not saved, seek the Lord, and get saved. If you are not in a Church, find a local church that reads the Holy Bible word for word, verse by verse, for Jesus Christ is my Lord and Savior, He is my healer, He is my deliverance from evil, The Lord is my provider, and most importantly He is my Father! Amen. As a church body, we need to stand in unity in these harsh times, to encourage one another, to lift the fallen, and to help the needy. Do more of God's Will and less of ours. Through the Blood of Jesus, we are victors, and victorious because of what He did for us all. We as descendants of Abraham must fight to keep the victory in Christ Jesus!

I pray for salvation and Healing for All, every nation, every gender, and every race.

> *"But my God shall supply all your needs according to his riches in glory by Christ Jesus"* (Philippians 4:19)

With the love of the Lord,
Jonathan L. Taylor

CHAPTER 2
THE LORD'S PERFECT PAINTING

Jonathan Taylor
March 26, 2016

Thus, it begins an amazing testimony of God's glory backed by the scripture of *"Give, and it shall be given to you. A good measure, pressed down, shaken together, and running over, will be poured into your lap. For with the measure you use, it will be measured to you".* **(Luke 6:38)**

This amazing story takes place here in Floresville, Texas, following the year before having given thy home to the Lord I still had many struggles to overcome. I was living in a tool shed on the property, but still I was being led by God's will. I lived in this tool shed for over a year with an outside shower and toilet, it was pretty difficult for me. My living conditions, attending Church, running my own business, and trying every day to tame the 13 acres I was living on, was tough. I had decided to get something I had wanted a very long time, yes, a Jeep. With that in mind, I was saving up the best I could despite my living conditions to buy a 1996 Jeep Wrangler. "Can you see where my priorities were?" However, I really desired something fun, for days or even weeks, to search night and day aimlessly on the internet for a jeep in my budget range.

After many hours spent searching for this said Jeep, at around 2 am,
I heard the Lord speak, "This one, He said!"
(Roman 10:17) states *"So, faith comes from hearing through the word of Christ",* Amen.

So, in my confusion, I scrolled and passed the Jeep I was told to be the one. I kept second-guessing what I heard. Later that morning I had already decided, about 6 am, that this Jeep was the one for me. Without hesitation, I was determined to get this Jeep at all cost. I went into my small safe and kept counting all the money I had saved for months. I must have counted it at least five to end up with $6,000 total, but the price listed was $7,500. I was still determined to buy it and the best I could do was offer a business check for $1,000. It was all I had left to my name, but I would still be $500 short. I was sure that most they would accept the $7,000. At this point, without speaking to the seller, I loaded up my big trailer and headed to our church daycare "Giggles n Slimes Learning Center" to make some repairs. I texted the seller and asked if that morning would work for him and as I was finishing the repairs, he responded and said yes, he could show me the vehicle that morning. I just had to let him know when I got into town. But little did he know, I intended to bring it back with me at all costs being that Pearsall, Texas, is approximately 80 miles from Floresville.

The Journey Begins

I headed out of Floresville, with a large trailer and $6,000 in cash, not knowing who I was going to meet. You can bet I was a bit uncomfortable. I chose to take all the back roads and enjoy the scenery with the music off and windows down, giving the good Lord thanks for the said day. Then the Lord spoke, "minister to him." I pondered what I had heard, and I had no clue as to whom I was going to meet, and who was I to minister to anyone? What would I say? How would I start the conversation with a complete stranger whom I had never met? I'm not ordained by a man and I carry no ministry degree, who am I to minister His word? All these thoughts had been crossing my mind.

(John 15:16) *"Ye have not chosen me, but I have chosen you, and ordained you, that ye should go and bring forth fruit"*. Amen.

As I entered Pearsall, the gentleman said to meet up with him at a gas station, with $6,000 in my pocket I, as you can bet, was a bit uncomfortable. So, we met, and I had mentioned something the Lord had shown me in a previous vision or dream I should say. The man was baffled. He told me that I had just confirmed questions that he had regarding the Holy Bible, and he had only attended his first three-week Bible study. *W*ow, that was amazing. I had no idea.

God is amazing and will use whom he wishes to spread his word. Little did I know, that would be *ME*. The man and I talked for quite some time, well over an hour, almost forgetting that I was there to purchase the jeep. After taking it for a drive and knowing it had a few issues, I still wanted to buy the Jeep. The gentleman agreed on 7k, but I had 6k cash and offered a business check for the remaining one thousand. He was very hesitant and did not want to accept a check. I mentioned to him that we can have your bank confirm the check. Little did I know the man was a Banker! He invited me to his office at the bank in which he worked. As it seemed to be an hour awaiting him to confirm the check, he finally said, OK, and you have 6k cash? I said yes and pulled it from my short's pockets. In disbelief that I had the cash on me, he called over one of the tellers. She counted the money to herself several times and kept looking at me in astonishment. Then called over another teller and had someone else count it. The entire bank was quiet at that time, and you could have heard a pin drop, she said," but sir this is not the 6k you said you have, it's 7K!" "Wow", I said aloud, Thank You, Jesus! Everybody in the bank knew that God's mighty hand had just moved*, as there was no way I* miscounted my funds and was off by one thousand dollars! Wow, boy, does God provide!

And my God will supply every need of yours according to his riches in glory in Christ Jesus. (Philippians 4:19)

The Perfect Painting

    I had spent a few months working on the Jeep, getting it the way, I wanted it. I installed a lift kit, tune-up, new gears, a positraction differential, a new clutch, a new transition, and lots of other new things. Finally, it was finished, exactly how I wanted it, though I had no clue that God had bigger plans for it. 2016 was the first year we were in our new Church, Floresville Christian Fellowship Church, and we planned to have an Easter carnival to raise funds for the parking lot we still do not have. At that time, I had given so much, done so much, not just for others, but for the Lord's house, just the same. *My pastor had called me a week before setting up this event to ask me to help with something.* Unfortunately, due to my exhaustion and frustration with helping so much, *I had lost my patience and spouted off, saying how I was just sick of helping and never to ask me to help again.* I wish I had not responded in the manner I had, but what was done was done.

The same day I was outside watering a pepper planter I had and not keeping in mind whatsoever the upcoming church event. I turned and looked at the Jeep and in the blink of an eye God himself had stopped time and space. I saw what looked like a painting canvas and all colors swirled in a mixing motion. I stood there in amazement of what I was shown, I saw exactly three days ahead of what I was to do for Him.

(Acts 2:22) ***"Men of Israel, listen to these words: Jesus the Nazarene, a man attested to you by God with miracles and wonders and signs which God performed through Him in your midst, just as you yourselves know"***. Amen.

I saw that I was to raffle off the Jeep to help with donations for our church parking lot. Though I fully did not understand, I came into an agreement with The Lord and said OK, done, I shall do what I had been shown. The next morning, as I headed to work at 4 am, I continued debating how could I donate this Jeep. I had just put $4,000 on a credit card to pay for the clutch and new transmission. Man, I just cannot totally lose on this. So, I said aloud, "I will split all proceeds with your house," the Lord spoke and said, "I'll match that half." Not knowing what that could exactly mean, *I was determined to do just that!*

After my job that morning, I headed off to the business where I have all my company shirts and invoices made. I then printed out 100 tickets at one hundred dollars each. At least if all the tickets were sold, I would have half to cover my credit card charges. When I got home, I cleaned up the 96 Jeep Wrangler with only 130k miles on it, in pristine condition, and drove to my Church. Parking in front of our Church, where the carnival was being set up and gave the tickets to my pastors. "Here, this is what I am doing," after I said that I was doing absolutely nothing. My Jeep was being raffled. Pastor and other church brothers had concerns that maybe, this indeed was too much giving. The year before, I had blessed my half-brother with my Titan so he could keep his job. I had given another church brother my dually because his vehicle kept going out. All of which have amazing testimonies in themselves. I still had my work truck, so all was still good because God is good! Thus, kicks off an even more amazing testimony of, Give, and it shall be given to you.

Raffle of the Jeep

I still ended up helping with the carnival and other things going on around the Church by helping cook the BBQ and such. I got to know a new church member that had just started attending with his wife and kids. All things aside, I was getting a bit upset knowing that only 30 tickets were sold, so with that in mind, I left out early before the drawing so that I would not see who would drive the Jeep away. The following morning as I waited in the church parking lot for Sunday service, that same gentleman was there with his family. He approached me and said, "I knew I was to win that Jeep." I responded with, "Well, how in the world could you have known that?" He told me of how he lost his Father eight years prior and how his Father willed him his Jeep. "OK," I said, "but what does a jeep being willed to you have to do with this Jeep being raffled?" As he explained, his sister got into a bind two years after they lost their dad, and she lost her vehicle, so he gifted her the Jeep his dad had willed him. "Wow", I said, he gifted a jeep, only to win one back years later in a raffle. That is amazing and only God could arrange such an amazing testimony and to use someone like me to be part of something so great.

(Isaiah 55:8-9) *"For MY thoughts are not your thoughts,"* declares the Lord. *"For as the heavens are higher than the earth, so are MY ways higher than your ways and MY thoughts than your thoughts."* Amen.

There was not much money gained for the Church; if it had not been for half of the raffle to His house, we would have been negative due to how expensive it was to have the carnival. But that is OK, for this amazing testimony is and forever will be such a great thing! The gentleman was even more amazed because he searched for an old vehicle to teach his son how to drive a standard. He was reluctant to buy one due to the possibility of the son burning out the clutch. He was so happy, so he said, "this jeep has a new clutch and transmission, and I can now teach my son." That is beautiful!

To conclude this testimony of how great God is, from start to finish, three days after church service, I had a side air condition job. The customer was someone I had known for a long time. At that time, she was one year sober and saved in the Lord Christ. As she kept trying to write the check for me, she kept saying, "This amount is not correct. I'm supposed to give you more." Being the honest man, I am, I could not urge her to give me more. I told her I would be grateful for more, but that is between you and God. She would not take no for an answer, so I said, "well, just add $300." She was still hesitant, saying "I think it is supposed to be $3,000." After all the years that I helped her and her husband, I would not allow that, so she agreed on the extra $300. Later that day, I did the math on how much I had made on that job; it was exactly the same dollar amount as the half of the raffle I blessed the Church in giving.

Wow, that's how God works! Be blessed, keep being a good steward of what God gives you,

"I have shown you all things, how that so laboring ye ought to support the weak, and to remember the words of Lord Jesus, how he said, It is more blessed to give than to receive" (Acts 20:35)

Written with the Love of Christ,
Jonathan Taylor.

CHAPTER 3
RESTORED FAITH

Jonathan Taylor
April 13, 2019

This is an amazing testimony of a woman's struggle and heroism to push forward in life, no matter how difficult life is, and surely it can be! **(Proverbs 18:10)** *"The name of the Lord is a strong tower; the righteous run into it and are safe"*, Amen.

A woman here in Sutherland Springs, Texas, by the name of Lisa McNulty, whom I have known and helped for several years around her home, doing miscellaneous and helping with repairs. For many years, she ran a dog rescue kennel at her home with about seventy-plus dogs and taking in abandoned animals with health issues, and finding homes for the ones she can, for surely the love of animals she has! Her amazing testimony begins several years before this day. About a year or so ago, she had battled colon cancer. Thank you, God, for her healing.

(Isaiah 53:5) *"But he was pierced for our transgressions, he was crushed for our iniquities; the punishment that brought us peace was on him, and by his wounds, we are healed"*. Amen, thank you, God, for our healings!

Lisa surely had more struggles to overcome, in the events that were to come. Who would have known that the upcoming attack on the Church there in Sutherland Springs, Texas would take place? Many lives were taken, and all lives would be changed forever! In this unfortunate event, Lisa McNulty's daughter, Terra McNulty, life was taken on that day. Lisa's two grandkids, James and Hailey, were both injured. With that said, Lisa's struggle got even more difficult! Man, if things were not bad enough. I pray for those taken and those who have lost so many, and those forever changed!

"Come to me, all you who are weary and burdened, and I will give you rest" (Matthew 11:28)

Amen and thank you, Jesus!

Things are tough, but we must not lose sight of our Lord and Savior! As you can imagine, the hurt, pain, and struggle from these sad events, caused Lisa to turn from the Church. She was hurt and unforgiving, seeing a new 3.5-million-dollar church being built. She now has adopted her grandchildren and still has not been given any financial support from all the donations. Even though it was not the Church's fault, anyone could only imagine the hurt from how that would look. ("A new church built, and my family and I still suffer"). It is understandable how anyone would turn away from Church or even God, for I may have done the same thing. Prayers out to those who have lost and will continue to suffer, Amen!

People in these situations, when bad things happen at Church want to blame God, asking why He did not stop what happened. Please keep in mind that God gives us free will, making the right decisions, and even bad ones. Bad choices have consequences, unfortunately, but our Heavenly Father is a God of correction and forgiveness.

"For if you forgive other people when they sin against you, your heavenly Father will also forgive you". (Matthew 6:14)

A Blessing in the Works

About a week before Palm Sunday, a gentleman by the name of Mike Greer approached me. He did not know God and wanted to find ways to help and bless people, as I had been doing for several years at this point. Mike had known me for many years. He did not understand my walk-in faith, although he saw and understand that the work, I was doing by blessing others were bringing blessing me. He wanted to find a way to help someone with a possible air condition system installation. We are both A/C contractors. Mike received approval from his distributor for a donation of said equipment providing that the people he helped were part of a charity. I kept in mind that a person's first time stepping up to help somebody is big. It is important to see who is being helped and see how they deserve the blessing, which would motivate Mike to do more of God's will. At that exact time, I didn't know of a charity nor an organization to direct him better.

The following morning at around 2 a.m., I was woken when, I heard the Lord speak to me and said, "Lisa!" Later that day, I was so determined to make sure Lisa was to receive a new A/C system. I had been maintaining her system for several years, knowing that it surely was on its last year. When I contacted Mike regarding Lisa needing this system, he said that his equipment supplier will most likely donate equipment in good faith. Unfortunately, only if she was part of some kind of actual charity organization. I told him that regardless of what needs to happen, I would max out my credit card if need be to ensure she gets a system. Mike decided he would go to his storage unit and see what equipment he had sitting there. Since I knew that Lisa had a 4-ton A/C system, I said we were to install a 5 ton! Mike was a little deterred, knowing he had just used the only 5-ton unit. As he checked his inventory, he called me baffled, saying, I know I had only one and used it, but there is a 5-ton outside condenser unit sitting right here... NEW... Wow, I knew at that point that God was behind this blessing!

"Give, and it shall be given to you" (Luke 6:38)

Knowing that Mike has the outside condenser unit, he said that he would donate it if I wanted to use his account to purchase the inside unit. As I set out to pick up the rest of the equipment, I was a bit detached, knowing my bank account was running pretty low. But as I purchased it, the actual dollar amount of what the unit would cost was EXACTLY what was in my bank account. Then I heard the Lord speak, "I Told You I Have This," which was amazing to hear, so I rejoiced in how good God is! All this was on a Wednesday, and so I had texted Lisa, seeing if she would mind if I were to bless her with a free A/C system tune-up. I could tell by her response that she was so excited to know her system was getting a tune-up before summer hit!

The Blessing

Little did Lisa know that a new system, was on the way, FREE! By Thursday, I had arranged for my 81-year-old grandfather, a retired A/C guy, my half-brother, who completed an A/C training course, and two of my church brothers to assist. They had helped me before installing a few A/C systems. At this point, I had a total of 6 men arranged to be at my house by 6 a.m. on a Saturday and I would have a huge complete meal cooked and awaiting. Being the funny guy, I am, I would not tell them why I needed them there, other than I was in desperate need of help at my house. So beautiful this was becoming, such a huge blessing waiting to unfold. When they arrived, I had explained Lisa's struggle, losing her daughter, having to adopt both grandkids, and struggling with taking them to rehab and therapy. Truly they were all moved as to how beautiful this blessing was going to be.

Miss Lisa knows how super early I get my day started. Lisa said, "You better not be here before 7:30 a.m. to service my system." At exactly 7:30 a.m., we showed up in several vehicles to get started. As we all pulled up, she was a little nervous, saying, "I really don't think it takes all these people to do what you said you were going to do." I introduced Mike and said, "on behalf of Mike, his Air Conditioning Company and Floresville Christian Fellowship, we are blessing you with a new 5-ton a/c system for free!" She was unable to compute what was going on at that moment and just said, "What do I need to do?" All I could say, in my funny humor, was, "just stay out of our way, woman!"

Some people understand how faith works, or should I say, God. But on the other hand, **people can see, feel, and recognize good deeds or works,** if you will. **But someone will say,**
"You have faith, and I have Work's" (James 2:18)
Show me your faith without your works, and I will show you my faith by my works. Amen. I continually sobbed, for days leading up to this amazing blessing, seeing how beautiful this was going to be. But how would I present this to her without making it about me, or my company? Do I mention God? Do I mention Church? How would she react? With these things in mind, I choose to just lead by good works, until after we wrapped up the job. After several hours of installation of the system, I had decided to gather all those who had helped in the front yard to pray for Lisa and the kid's restoration, guidance, and protection. And the best thing I could find to say to her was, "I hope this restores not just your faith in God, but your faith in Church because this is what it should look like." I was sorry to say, and I wished someone had done this for you all sooner! That was just perfect! Thank you, God, for the wisdom and guidance to understand and consider people's emotions.

Restored Faith

I am truly blessed to be a partaker in this HUGE blessing and uplifting in someone's life. Little did I know that the Saturday we had installed this system was the night or her was the granddaughter's prom and Sunday was Palm Sunday. Wow how amazing it is. God's timing has been so perfect. Even *more surprising was when I read* on Facebook about how happy Lisa was! Having said, "I have finally found a church that isn't greedy and how she had finally found a home." What moved me, even more was her excitement in saying "that I am stepping back into the Church with both my kids," and she sure did. The first day back was Mother's Day March 12, 2019. Thank God! I was obedient to God as all of us men were and even better, Mike Greer as of February 5, 2020, started into the Church!

I am grateful for being a part of God's testimony, uplifting those who truly need it. I pray others to follow, not just leading people into Church but to be of a giving heart. A doer of His Works and His Will.

"Knowing that whatsoever good thing any man doeth, the same shall he receive of the Lord, whether he bond or free"
(Ephesians 6:8) Amen.

Written with the love and compassion of Christ,
Jonathan Taylor
March 1, 2020

CHAPTER 4
A BOOST OF FAITH

Jonathan Taylor
June 5, 2018

This testimony takes place in Floresville, Texas at Floresville Christian Fellowship Church with an amazing servant and warrior of God, Susi Manfredi, and her struggle of being diagnosed with stage 4 cancer. As Sister Susi had said at the altar, I will not be cut on nor operated on, and by His stripes, I shall be healed!

"And by His stripes, we are healed"
(Isaiah 53:5) Amen.

It is not easy to deal with these struggles, especially when the doctors told her she only had 3-4 months to live. Boy, did they underestimate God's power! Susi, being a nurse and her husband an EMT, already knew the struggle that laid ahead of them since they had several children. Tough most definitely, no matter who you are. As a church, we had ignited in prayer, helping, and uplifting them the best we could. By no means did she allow them to cut on her. She did have to get chemo to help cope with the brutal pain she endured.

I have my struggles in life. Even choosing to purchase a 2012 Ducati Monster Evo 1100 street bike, by far the most fun, and dangerous motorcycle "bike," I had ever owned. I am kind of "Evil Knievel" kind of guy, probably had no business with such a toy. But little did I know God had bigger plans for the bike. Being a good steward of what is God's is extremely important in life. In essence, all things belong to God, including us.

"Moreover, it is required in stewards that a man be found faithful" (1 Corinthians 4:2)

I was outside watering my grass one day, and I heard the Lord speak and say, "Mark and Bike." I knew Sister Susi's husband's name was Mark. Right there at that moment I agreed and said, "Done, I will bless Brother Mark with the bike." I was unclear as to why the Lord had asked me to do that, as I was already trying to figure out the testimony before it had come to be. My thinking was they needed extra money, either way, it was doing a good deed, and surely God would still bless me for blessing them.

The Church members knew that Brother Mark was an avid bike rider, so maybe this bike being in his hands would uplift things. Little did I know what this single act of obedience was going to do for him and his family? It was funny to picture Brother Mark on the bike as he is a large man. I was hoping to gift him the bike in a Sunday church service, but unfortunately, he had to work that day. Instead, I had called him to explain how the Lord had asked me to gift him this awesome bike. His response was that of, "no, I don't think so, and I will not accept that from you." My answer as the funny guy was, "well, your bike is here on church property, and if you don't come and pick it up, we are having it towed off!" Big words coming from a small guy like me. He then said, "You are really doing me like this"? I said it is done. Even though you are going through "hell," God is still good in the middle of your hell!

The Blessing at Work

It was several days before he had picked up the motorcycle and was about a week later when we had spoken. To my amazement, I was starting to see how the blessing was at work. As we talked, Brother Mike told me that this Ducati was a real desire of his heart and how he always wanted that exact bike above the ones he had. *Wow*, I had no clue, but surely God knew!

"Delight thyself also in the Lord, and He shall give thee the desires of the heart" (Psalms 37:4) Amen.

Our conversation continued and he told me exactly what the bike did for him; one morning, with everyone inside asleep, he decided to give up on the fight and struggles. He could no longer watch his wife and family suffer, so he had packed a bag and was heading to his garage to jump on one of his bikes and hit the road and never look back, back to his previous ways of a biker living on the go. But as he entered and saw this, he was blown away by the fact that If God loves me this much to place a desire of my heart here in one of the darkest times of my life, surely this struggle is nothing! So, he stayed to carry out the battle alongside his wife.

The following week in church service, I was confronted by Sister Susi. She thanked me for being obedient to God and blessing her husband. She told me her husband had a maintenance log sheet on the garage wall with their cars, bikes, lawnmowers, and such. That page had only one empty line. For some time, her husband said that one day he would have that bike on it, and low and behold, there it is. That is so amazing how this testimony was coming together, in God's perfect timing in this and using me as a sinner, an ordinary person, nobody, to be part of something so amazing. Though we do not always know what God is doing, I assure you that His ways are better, and in being obedient, we become more blessed.

> **"*I can be a blessing in that way, even though they may never know that I am praying for them. If I see a need, then I need to be faithful to be a 'servant of all"* (Ezekiel 22:30)**
> Such a perfect scripture.

After the struggles they had endured, eight months later, keeping in mind the docs saying she had only three months, yes, she got on chemo due to the pain endured. Still, as she vowed, they did not operate on her whatsoever. And after a follow visit, *Cancer Free!* Amen, Glory to God in the Highest! Praise God for her belief, as she never gave up, she was in almost all church services, and despite her struggles, she always kept joy, hope, and praise on her lips. And she to this day is still alive and serving in our Church, as a living testimony of how great God is. I say to all of you struggling out there in the world, for we all have struggles, and I encourage you through your struggles to put God first and see what He will do for you, through you, and all around you. For only faith, that of a mustard seed can truly move the mountains of struggle. Amen and God Bless you ALL!

"Jesus said, "Because you have so little faith" (Matthew 17:20)

Truly I tell you, if you have faith like a grain of mustard seed, you can say to this mountain, 'Move from here to there,' and it will move. Nothing will be impossible for you.

Written with the love of Christ,

Jonathan Taylor

Just One Step
Jonathan Taylor

It hit me one day as I ministered to a customer who just could not get through one more day. In an adjacent perspective, I used football to demonstrate a point of continuing forward. The vision given to me was that of, how are Football Games Won? Touchdowns! But how do you gain a touchdown/goal? One yard at a time! Put this concept into God's plan, life's plan. If we stop and give up, we gain no yardage. The "Touchdown" in my perspective is HEAVEN! Our every step taken, and every yard gained gets us closer to Heaven and that is Our TRUE Touchdown! Though we may fumble, backslide, or even just stop or give up, keep in mind if all we can do is gain one step forward in this one day, then We Have Gained another step closer to Heaven! Keep marching forward! **Do not Give Up** and whatever you do, **Don't Look Back**. Keep All Focus on that "Touchdown" of Heaven!

Roughly about July 10, 2017, I fell into a pit of depression and being alone as usual, I was falling apart. That morning I decided I would not do anything, stay in bed, *something I never do,* and just *give up*! I started going back to sleep at about 7 am. I heard a loud growl that would wake anyone! Then the Good Lord spoke, "you have been encouraging my children by giving them hope of, Just Gain One Yard, One step, if that's all you can do!" Then he told me, "at least take one step!" So as I struggled to gain my one step for an entire day, I went to my Church, His Tent, His House, **For I Am HIS PEOPLE** and completed, at least one flaw of the new construction of His House.

When I finished doing just that one thing, the Lord told me: "YOU GAINED ONE YARD!" AMEN, Thank You, Father Jesus

Written on this August 2, 2017
With the Love of Christ

CHAPTER 5
UPLIFTING OF HOPE

An uplifting of hope occurs here at Floresville Christian Fellowship Church in Floresville, Texas, that involves our now head usher, Brother Tino Talamantez. In the year 2017, our pastors were out on a mission trip. I was opening the Church and overseeing church services at that time. Knowing Brother Tino had gone through an unfortunate divorce, struggled, got a new job, and had for the first time in his life received Jesus Christ as his Lord and Savior at about the age of 58. Tough times were upon him, and surely everyone could understand this. Especially with having a young daughter about thirteen years old and two sons of about eighteen. In the Sunday service, he mentioned that he would need to be leaving services early that morning for personal reasons. As Tino began to go, I stopped him and asked how he was doing, boy I had no idea what I was walking into at that time.

Brother Tino had mentioned that his son's car was down and that he had to shuttle them around so that they all could still maintain their jobs. That was hard on him due to him having just got hired at VP Racing. As he told me, his ex-father-in-law is on his deathbed. If I have to give up my new job so that my sons can keep their jobs and take my car so they can move forward in life, so be it, I will wait by my in-law's bedside till he passes and figure out what to do then. What touched me is that he said that he may be missing church services and how here is where he wants to be! *Wow,* that's bold and genuinely a father's love for his sons!

"For God so loved the world that he gave his one and only son, that whoever believes in him shall not perish but have everlasting life" (John 3:16) Amen.

This knowledge touched my heart. About two months prior, I had purchased a "hot rod" for a project fun car, 1996 Chevy Camaro that had a new 383 stroker motor. I had just gotten it all fixed up, running very excellent. That night, as I pondered his struggles and if I did nothing, would he quit coming to Church and fall back into his old ways, how bad I would feel. In perspective, I had a "key" that could set him free of his cell and his problems. It just so happened, to be indeed a key, and as a people, if we have a "key" to set someone else free of their struggles and burdens, who are we not to set them free? Jesus Christ sets us free, and He saves us from sin and death.

"Salvation is found in no one else, for there is no other name under Heaven given to mankind by which we must be saved"
(Acts 4:12).

I had a decision to make, do I bless him with the car I just got for myself, or do I watch them find their way? Truly I deserved the car. Before this one, I had blessed other vehicles in the number of roughly three or four. Still, by making an unselfish gesture of love and compassion for a struggling family when I am a family of just one, this could set them free.

A Blessing in the Works

That evening as I sat admiring a cool vehicle that I had just completed; I knew what I had to do. Bless Brother Tino with this Camaro and stand back to see what God will do in their lives. We are called to be good stewards of what is God's. In essence, this world and everything in it, including ourselves, belongs to God.

"Moreover, it is required in stewards that a man is found faithful" (1 Corinthians 4:2). Amen.

The following morning at roughly 6:00 a.m., as I was doing some repairs at a restaurant that I worked for, knowing he would pass by. I called him, telling him that I had to talk to him immediately before he arrived at work. He was a bit hesitant in stopping but finally agreed to, for what I had to say would only take a minute.

At about 6:30 a.m., Tino stopped by where I was working. As he approached me I said to him, as I held out my hand with a set of car keys, "Here. Now there is no reason as to why you cannot keep your job, and your sons keep their jobs. You can be at every church service!" He was great and the joy I saw in him even after his Father-in-law passed. He was so uplifted with joy, praise, and happiness. As of May 3, 2020, he still has his job, attends almost all church functions, and is deemed our head usher here at our Church. Praise God for glory be His!

"Give, and it will be given to you" (Luke 6:38).

A good measure, pressed down, shaken together, and running over, will be poured into your lap. For with the measure you use, it will be measured to you. I encourage you, help others the best you can in these trying times, and watch what God will do for you. Amen

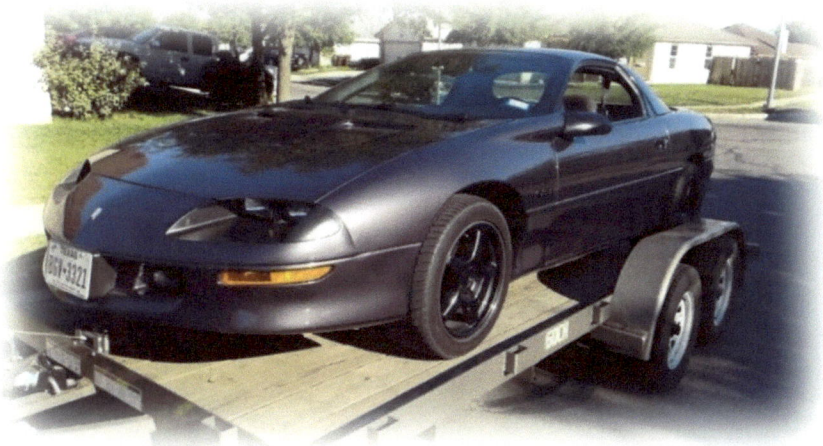

A Deserved Blessing

This testimony starts from the day that our new Church, Floresville Christian Fellowship, was being built around 2016 and involves a church Brother Cory Kernen. In this testimony, I will share this man's sacrifice and dedication to helping not just the Lord's people but also the aiding in the building of several churches, including this Church. Though this is his testimony, I would like to write about it because I have been part of it twice in this time. In 2014, Cory was led to Floresville, Texas and lived with our pastors for a while, while he served our Church and our church's learning center, Giggles and Smiles. During this time, he helped with the repairs and maintenance of the center. He has often helped the needy and the elderly with small home repairs and even auto mechanic work, due to people being unable to pay companies to do such things.

We were at the time still having Church service in the same building as the daycare. Cory had mentioned that his car had gone out during one service. He asked that if anybody knew of someone selling a car, to please let him know. At that moment, I heard the Lord speak to me, "Give him your keys." What, really? I have just given my home, fully furnished, through Church to a needy family. I was currently living in a tool shed due to this on 13 acres that I had just purchased. Not only that, but I had just blessed a half-brother of mine my Nissan Titan because he had just lost his vehicle and had his first good paying job in his life in the oil field. During this time, I had bought an awesome big truck, and the Lord wanted me to bless him with it after everything I had just sacrificed. Naturally, the answer was no, even though I had a work truck so I would not be left without a vehicle. But my answer was still like, no, no, I do not think so... For weeks, every time I looked at the truck, I would hear, "call him and give it to him."

Corinthians 9:6-8 says, "*each of you should give what you have decided in your heart to give, not reluctantly or under compulsion, for God loves a cheerful giver, and God can bless you abundantly, so that in all things at all times, you will abound in every good work.*" Amen!

It may have been two months or so later when was outside one day having an "adult beverage" and glanced at the truck. Yet again I heard, "call him and give him the truck." Out of frustration and being stubborn as usual, I threw my drink and yelled out loud, "fine because if I call him and do this then, you can't bother me anymore!" So, without hesitation, I called Brother Cory and said, "This truck is yours." Even funnier he was like "OK, I will be right there," with no hesitation in his voice or surprise. I asked him, "You knew this truck was going to be yours, didn't you?" He said, "Yes, the Lord said it was mine." Being the hard-headed man, I am, I said "but you didn't know when you were going to get it through, did you?" He said "nope." To bless Cory even more abundantly, I decided to also give him also my 18' dual axle trailer. This way Cory would have the tools to help him and bless others more. If this story is not great enough, the next week on Facebook, I saw he had towed someone's car that had broken down so that he could fix it for them. Even greater, the following weeks, the truck and trailer were used to haul equipment and materials, which aided in the finishing of our new Church here in Floresville, TX. Amen and Thank You, Father.

About a year after we were in our new Church, I had bought a 1988 Mustang GT convertible, for I enjoy building Hot Rods and driving them. I had desired a 1965 Mustang since I had childhood memories of my dad racing them, but at the time, I could not afford it. I compromised and settled for the 88. I had spent the next three years building this car, replacing everything under it, including a new 331 stroker motor and transmission. I went a bit overboard on this build by installing a supercharger and even an entirely new computer system. Go big or go home, so I was going big at home. This Mustang is such a fun 500 horsepower car. I had it almost repainted, new tires, and lots of other new stuff. Again, the Lord had other plans for this car, though my heart was set on having this '65 Mustang!

Around March of 2020, as I was sitting outside chilling, enjoying my property, I heard the Lord so lightly speak and say, "Cory and Car." As I gazed upon the "Hot Rod" that was virtually 95 percent redone, I said "yes and Amen." As I texted brother Cory and told him, "This car is yours." He knew of all my blessings and sacrifices, so his response was, "I do not deserve that car!" That night as I pondered that idea, does he deserve it? I knew that he was an adopted child, mid 40's, and had been serving our Heavenly Father since around age seventeen for most of his life. I did not know until recently that he moved from state to state for years!

Everywhere Cory moved, God always placed him where a new church was being built. A single, unmarried man, moving around to help build several churches from start to finish, living with pastors, working for pretty much minimum wage. It is difficult for him to have nice things and his own home or a new car was pretty much out of the question.

Brother Cory was placed here in Floresville, Texas, about 2015 and served in our old Church, even in our church daycare over the years and spent countless hours assisting in the building of our new Church. Around 2018, he had decided to leave our Church and moved to the opposite side of San Antonio, Texas. He, by trade, is a heavy equipment operator. He went to work full time, establishing his place to live and working a lot to achieve greater things in life. Quite frankly, it is nice to have beautiful things in life, though possessions are not everything, they are nice to have; in essence, in life, God is all we truly need.

"You, Lord are all I have, and you give me all I need; my future is in your hands" (Psalms 16:5). Amen.

In closing this fantastic testimony, when I was in Church that following Sunday, The Lord spoke to me and said, "Yes, it was ME that asked you to do that for my son." My childhood response was, "I thought I was your son." FYI that is how I act often. Nonetheless, the Lord said, "you are my son, but do you have any idea what was done for my son?" I said, "Well, Cory probably feels happy, uplifted, and loved." I do not know since about eight years now, I generally, do not feel those things due to living alone for such a long time. I could not imagine how that would feel to be blessed with something so cool for free, knowing it is sent from our Heavenly Father. At that exact moment, the Lord hit me with Brother Cory's joy! Boom, and instantly I laughed, smiled, and felt joy, his happiness. That lasted only for a moment, but at that very moment, I felt all those things I generally never feel. Thank you, God, for that moment, though I pray I have more of those moments not just in my life but in everyone.

Nehemiah 8:10 *"Do not grieve, for the joy of the Lord is your strength".* Amen.

I have a difficult time being "obedient" to what the Holy Spirit of God asks me to do, though these things are done. I find it tough because nothing is given to me by anyone. Honestly, I am not a rich man of finance. I set out, work hard for the things I would like to have, and apparently, the Lord has more significant ideas than my own as to whom the items genuinely belong. But, in this instance God said to me loudly in service, "because of what you placed in my son's lap, I will put something in yours. That all you will need to do is to reach out and take it, for what you placed in his lap, I will place in yours!" Wow, Amen! Still, on this said day of May 3, 2020, I await impatiently, as to what the Lord will be doing for me, nor can I wait to write the fantastic testimony when the time comes. To all I say, do not grow weary of doing good deeds for the Lord in His mighty name! He will do something for you; keep in mind that it may be something you can or cannot see. He very well may have prevented a major catastrophe in your life or has got you through one. Keep your faith, keep pushing forward in a Heavenly direction, and watch what God will do for you!

"Truly, I tell you, if you have faith as small as a mustard seed, you can say to this mountain, ' Move from here to there, ' and it will move. Nothing will be impossible for you" (Matthew 17:20).
Amen, though, if it is His will for you!

Written with the Love and compassion of Christ,
Jonathan Taylor

Bible Verses to Study Guide

Forty scriptures are quoted in this book. Take the time to read the scriptures. My challenge to you is to see where Faith and Works apply to your life. May you have a Multitude of Blessings!

Chapter 1

Luke   6:38
Psalm   147:3
1 Corinthians 12:4
1 Corinthians 12:11
Matthew   19:26
Acts   2:4
Hebrews   4:12
Deuteronomy 15:10
Proverbs   21:26
Psalm   103:23
Ezekiel   37:7
Philippians   4:19

NOTES

Chapter 2

Luke	6:38
Romans	10:17
John	15:16
Philippians	4:19
Acts	2:22
Isaiah	55:8-9
Acts	20:35

NOTES

Chapter 3

Proverbs	18:10
Isaiah	53:5
Matthew	11:28
Matthew	6:14
James	2:18
Ephesians	6:18

NOTES

Chapter 4

Isaiah   53:5
1 Corinthians 4:2
Isaiah   53:5
Psalms   37:4
Ezekiel   22:30
Matthew   17:20

NOTES

Chapter 5

John	3:16
Acts	4:12
1Corinthians	4:20
Luke	6:38
2 Corinthians	9:6-8
Psalms	16:5
Nehemiah	8:10
Matthew	17:20
James	2:26

NOTES

With the love of Christ,

Jonathan Taylor

ABOUT THE AUTHOR

Jonathan Taylor, the founder of Precision Mechanical, self-employed since 2010, specializing in service and repair of heating, Air conditioning, refrigeration, ice machines, and restaurant cooking equipment.

He is a single man since 2012. His time spent mostly, seeking the Lord and dedication time to serving the Christian Fellowship Church, local community and providing an unexpected blessing to many along the way. God and the teachings of Jesus Christ have been the focus of his being. His mission is being charitable and servant the Heavenly Father. The testimonies in this book show obedience to Christ's teachings in the faithfulness of blessing others in many ways. Through the blessing of much, the power of the Lord and His glory is witnessed by many.

Jonathan lives outside of Floresville, Texas, in a home he built himself in his spare time over a period of five years, while clearing his thirteen-acre home site. His animal family consist of one dog, two cats, and fifteen chickens. These are his simple pleasures outside of the church until the Lord blesses him with the perfect mate.

www.ingramcontent.com/pod-product-compliance
Lightning Source LLC
Chambersburg PA
CBHW042042090426
42733CB00027B/51